# SOUTH AMERICA

Troll Associates

# SOUTH AMERICA

by Francene Sabin

Illustrated by Allan Eitzen

**Troll Associates**

*Library of Congress Cataloging in Publication Data*

Sabin, Francene.
    South America.

    Summary: A brief overview of South American
geography.
        1. South America—Description and travel—1981-
Juvenile literature. [1. South America—Geography]
I. Eitzen, Allan, ill. II. Title.
F2208.5.S22    1985        980        84-8586
ISBN 0-8167-0292-6 (lib. bdg.)
ISBN 0-8167-0293-4 (pbk.)

Imagine a place where no rain has fallen for hundreds of years...or a place where more than 200 inches of rain fall every year. How about a waterfall that's as tall as a thirty-story building? Imagine seeing a rodent as large as a Great Dane...or a school of razor-toothed fish that can strip the meat off an animal's bones in minutes! All these things are real, and they can be found on the continent of South America.

South America lies between the Atlantic Ocean, which is on the east, and the Pacific Ocean, which is on the west. To the north, the Caribbean Sea separates South America from North America. But the two continents are joined by a narrow strip of land known as Central America.

Andes Mountains

South America, the fourth largest continent on Earth, has three main regions. There is the mountain chain known as the Andes, which stretches along the west coast of South America for about 5,000 miles. It goes from the very northern end of the continent, in Venezuela, to the southern end, in Chile.

The Andes Mountains are rugged and high, with canyons almost twice as deep as North America's Grand Canyon. These mountains are in a zone of great underground activity. There are many live volcanoes that erupt from time to time, and there are frequent violent earthquakes.

10

The mountains in the east of the continent, called the highlands, are not as jagged as the Andes. They are low, rounded, rolling, green mountains. There are three sections of South America that are known as highlands. One, the Guiana Highlands, is located in the northeast part of the continent, in the countries of Venezuela, Guyana, Surinam, French Guiana, and the northern section of Brazil.

Guiana
Highlands

The second highland region is in the southern part of the continent—in Argentina. It is called Patagonia, and it is a cool and dry area used mainly for raising sheep.

The largest highland region is known as the Brazilian Highlands. It stretches more than 2,000 miles from the east coast of South

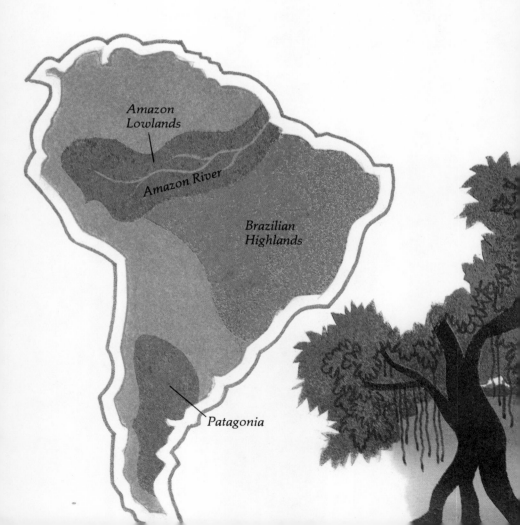

Amazon Lowlands

Amazon River

Brazilian Highlands

Patagonia

America almost to the Andes. The Brazilian Highlands are green and fertile, with many rivers and productive farm lands.

Just north of the Brazilian Highlands is the largest lowland area in South America. It is called the Amazon Lowlands. This area is a broad band of land reaching from the Andes all the way to the Atlantic Ocean.

The lowlands are kept green all year round by the Amazon River and its many tributaries. The Amazon is sometimes called the world's greatest river. That is because, together with its tributaries, the Amazon drains more territory than any other single river system. It also carries more water than any other river system in the world.

South America's other lowlands regions are called the Orinoco Llanos and the Argentine Pampa. The Llanos, in the northern part of the continent, and the Pampa, in the south, are both flat grasslands. But they are not at all alike.

The Llanos is so dry that few people live in it, and it has very little farming or industry. The Pampa is very much like the plains of the North American Midwest. Its rich soil, favorable climate, and moderate rainfall are ideal for growing grains and for raising cattle.

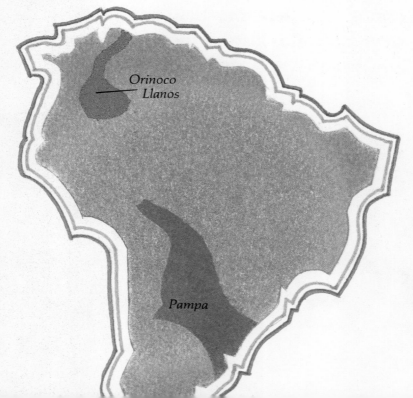

Orinoco
Llanos

Pampa

South America is better known for its rivers than its lakes. The only lake of note is Lake Titicaca, which is high in the Andes Mountains on the border of Peru and Bolivia. It is the highest lake in the world used by steamships.

The steamships that carry people and goods across the lake were built in England. Then they were sailed over many thousands of ocean miles to Peru. There, the steamships were taken apart and taken over the Andes by mules and railroad. At the lake, the steamships were reassembled.

Lake Titicaca is also the site of La Paz, the capital of Bolivia. It is more than two miles above sea level, which makes it the highest capital city on Earth.

There are five great river systems in South America. In addition to the Amazon, they are the Rió de la Plata system, the Magdalena and Cauca Rivers, the Orinoco, and the São Francisco. The Rió de la Plata system is the most important inland waterway on the continent. It is used extensively for the transportation of people and products.

Airplanes are also used for long-distance travel and transportation, because the dense South American rain forests make land transportation difficult. But the Pan American Highway joins the countries together, and good roads are also found in the larger cities. Railroads link many of the larger cities. In the rural countryside, however, there may be dirt roads or no roads at all.

The Amazon and Orinoco rain forests are so thick and humid that there are still sections that are unmapped. The Indian tribes that live in them exist as their ancestors did hundreds of years ago. They hunt, fish, and grow just enough food to feed themselves.

In order to plant crops, these Indians must first cut down and burn away a section of the heavy rain-forest vegetation. But this cleared land can be farmed for only a few years. Then the soil, which is not very fertile, will no longer produce good crops.

Rain-forest soil is poor because the trees, shrubs, and dense undergrowth use up most of the nutrients in the soil. That is why the tribes of the rain forest must move from place to place every few years. It is the only way they can survive.

The rain forests and the bone-dry South American deserts are equally difficult places in which to live. But much of South America is good farm land, producing coffee, fruit, sugar cane, cotton, grains, and cacao, which is used to make chocolate.

In addition, the grazing lands of South America produce a large share of the world's lamb and beef. And because the equator passes through South America, most of the continent is warm all year. This means there is a long growing season and an abundance of crops.

South America is rich in mineral resources, many of which have hardly been touched. For example, Bolivia is among the world's leading tin producers.

But mining the tin is difficult because the mines are high in the Andes Mountains. It is hard for the miners to breathe at the high altitudes because the air is so thin. It is also hard to ship machines and tools to the tin mines, and just as hard to ship out the ore.

In addition to tin, the countries of South America export bauxite to make aluminum, as well as copper, iron, zinc, lead, diamonds, emeralds, gold, silver, and nickel.

Venezuela is now one of the world's leading producers of oil. And several other South American countries have oil lands that are just beginning to be developed.

The continent of South America is also rich in wildlife. In the rain forests are several kinds of monkeys, as well as bats, porcupines, otters, ocelots, pumas, wild boars, jaguars, and a great variety of rodents, including the four-foot-long capybara.

And the Andes Mountains are home for the llama, a cousin of the camel. The llama is used to carry heavy loads, its wool is made into clothing, and its milk and meat provide food for Andean Indians.

The Andean Indians are among the many millions of people in South America who live in poverty and who lack medical care and education. In spite of the vast resources and wealth of South America, very little of it in the past has gone to help the people. But this is changing. Large plantations and unused lands are being divided among poor farmers by the governments of some South American countries.

Manufacturing is being encouraged in many South American countries. Until recently, such raw materials as metal ores and cotton were shipped elsewhere to be turned into finished products. Today, South American factories are beginning to process these raw materials. This provides jobs and helps the South American economy.

Today, most South Americans speak either Spanish or Portuguese, because the first explorers of the continent were from Spain and Portugal. These explorers first reached South America's shores about 500 years ago.

Since then, South America has faced great difficulties. It has seen its people suffer through centuries of slavery under its conquerors. It has seen its natural resources shipped out to benefit the people of other lands. And it has seen its native customs nearly stamped out.

But today, South America—the fourth largest continent in the world—is looking toward the future. It is made up mostly of independent countries, and each is working to expand its manufacturing and develop its resources. This continued economic development is one of the roads that South America is following as it moves away from its past and into the future.